The Grief Book

Debbie Moore

&

Carolyn Cowperthwaite

The Grief Book

ISBN-10: 1482688085
ISBN-13: 978-1482688085

To those people we have loved and lost and
to those we love now

Debbie Moore and Carolyn Cowperthwaite

Authors' Note

While the substance of each of the anecdotes used in the text is true, all identities have been disguised by changing names and other descriptive details.

The Grief Book

CONTENTS

The Grief Book

ABOUT THIS BOOK

You may have all sorts of reasons for reading this book – desperation, curiosity, simply because someone gave it to you and you don't want to hurt their feelings – but, in the end, at the root of it all, isn't there at least a little tiny part of you that wants to take control of your grief, to turn it into something that you can live with and learn from?

That's what this book is about – your very own particular grief, not anybody else's. We hope to help you to understand your own grief, to provide you with an array of tools to choose from to help you manage your grief in the **Bring joy and happiness back into your life** way that is best for you. We offer a selection of simple straightforward strategies to help you move through your grief to a better place, a place where you can bring joy and happiness back into your life.

We believe that there are as many different ways of grieving as there are people on this planet. We hope that we can help you to recognise and understand your own grief, to identify what is going on in your own life, and to provide you with some ideas to help you through. We want to show you how you have the ability to take control of your life IN THE WAY THAT SUITS YOU.

There are no magical steps of faith for you to take, simply try out some of the ideas and see if they work for you.

SECTION 1

Who are you?

From the devastation of loss comes grief. Grief is the normal reaction to loss. It can feel that life has been blown apart and when grieving we can lose our sense of who

> **Grief is the normal reaction to loss**

we are now. In this section we are going to consider who you actually are.

In the first chapter we will take a look at how grief can completely take over your life, how it can dominate and define you. We will think about what this means in practical terms for you in your life as it is right now, offering strategies to help cope with these sometimes overwhelming feelings.

Chapter Two will ask you to look at who you are now, after your loss. It is vital that you can

> **Find your true identity**

find your true identity in order to work out how to

carry on living. Knowing yourself will be your anchor to give you stability as you work through the turmoil of grief. We will ask you to think about who you are, who you would like to be and we will work on how to get your life back by considering ways in which you can reclaim your essential self and start rebuilding your life.

In Chapter Three we will examine how your relationships with other people are affected by grief, not only your grief but

> **Other people's expectations can drown out your own wants and needs**

their grief too. We will look at how other people can influence how you behave and how their expectations can drown out your own wants and needs. Ways of recognising and dealing with these relationships will be discussed.

CHAPTER ONE

A THOUSAND PIECES?

This is about you

You are grieving.

Someone close to you has died. You couldn't really imagine this finally happening, or perhaps you thought that you had come to terms with the possibility, accepted what was going to happen and had got to grips with it. However nothing really prepares you for the reality and the finality of death. Now it has happened, the person close to you has died and it hurts – badly, or perhaps, what can seem even worse, you feel totally numb when you think you should be hurting. You are in shock. However well prepared you thought you were, you didn't ever think that it was actually going to be today that it would happen, that your loved one really would die, and now it has. Your emotions may be all over the place or seem to be totally absent.

You are overwhelmed with grief and it dominates your life. In some way this event has broken your spirit. You may feel like you have been ripped into a thousand pieces. Or you may feel numb, locked in a glass box, completely separated from the rest of

You feel that you no longer have control of your life

the world. Whatever your state, you feel that you no longer have control of your life and you want to do something about it, otherwise you wouldn't have picked up this book.

We'd like to help you find ways of dealing with that hurt, that pain and that sorrow, to help you put yourself back together again. We are not guaranteeing to take away all the hurt but hope to show you how you can work through the pain to find moments of hope, of possibility and of joy so that you can move forward in your life.

Your grief

Someone close to you has died and this has had a

profound effect on your life. This is your loss. It's like nobody else's. You may be experiencing any or many of a wide range of emotions including anger that you have been left alone, guilt that you didn't do enough, or fear that others will be taken from you. Depression about the fragility of life may have swamped you, or perhaps you have become a complete party animal who can't bear to stay in and spend time on your own. Maybe you even have a feeling of relief that all the illness and anxiety is over with and you can get back to a normal life but something is stopping you living life to the full again.

Perhaps, however, you don't want to feel like this, to be overwhelmed by grief in whatever form it takes for you, for the rest of your life. Maybe you

> **You would like to take back control of your life**

have decided that it wouldn't be good for you or your family or your friends for you to continue like this, that you would like to take back control of your life and live how you choose.

Does this seem an impossible dream? We firmly believe that it isn't. Yes, you may always have the sorrow but it doesn't have to dominate your life. It may instead give you a different perspective on life as you learn from your experiences and rebuild your life without the person who has died. This book is all about the steps that you can take to heal yourself, to move forward and to get the life that you want.

The most difficult step

YOU HAVE ALREADY TAKEN THE MOST DIFFICULT STEP

– YOU HAVE STARTED READING THIS BOOK

It doesn't matter how you came by the book, whether you bought it yourself, were given it by a well-meaning friend, got it from the library, found it in a charity shop, or are even just browsing through it in a bookshop. No one could have forced you to open it. That was your choice and your first step on your journey. By opening this book and reading these words you have shown that you are interested in finding a way through your grief. No one else can find that for you.

Remember that you are in control.

You can do what you want with this book

- Read it in one go

- Read a bit each day

- Dip in and out as the mood takes you

- Put it down when you want to

- Throw it at the wall when you want to

- Put it in the back of a drawer

- Even throw it away – but please don't do that – give us a chance.

There is no right way or wrong way to use this book. You are unique and you know what is right for you. Remember:

THERE ARE NO RULES FOR GRIEF

Everybody's grief is unique. However you have reacted so far is fine, it's how you needed to be. There is no one correct way to grieve. There are as many different ways to grieve, as there are people grieving. And all of us need to grieve, to take time to mourn the loss of someone close to us. It is when that grief continues to dominate our lives and direct our actions, when it prevents us returning to a full and happy life, that we may want to find ways of managing that grief and moving forward.

In this chapter we try to provide you with a few

simple steps that might help you to set out along that path to a life that you can enjoy.

If you're not sure that you want to take a step at all, ask yourself why you picked up this book in the first place. Isn't that a sign that you want to change? Perhaps you could at least read the list of suggestions that follows at the end of this chapter? You might find something that appeals to you. Remember, you don't have to do anything if you don't want to. It's your life and your choice.

If you still don't feel ready, put this book in the back of the drawer again until you do [but don't forget that it's there!].

However, you may want to take one of those steps now. If so, read on.

Moving forward

In your current state you may feel broken physically, emotionally and mentally. Physically, your body reacts to grief in a number of ways. You may stop looking after your body the way you normally do. So, for example, you may find it very difficult to eat, or you may find that you are consoling yourself with food. Emotionally, it may seem that your feelings are all over the place, or they may seem absent altogether. You may cry a lot or never cry at all. As for the mental brokenness, you may find it difficult to think clearly, to organise your thoughts and actions, or you may find yourself obsessing over the smallest details in an attempt to win back control of your life. Individuals can react in such different ways from each other even when grieving over the loss of the same person.

Alison and Rob did just this following the death of their young son, Joe, who was 19 years old at the time of his death. Alison could not face seeing her friends or colleagues and she could not think straight enough to contemplate even going to work. Alison loved her job and had an extremely strong work ethic and yet she could not even talk about the possibility of returning to her job. Rob, on the other hand, decided he needed to return to work four days after the funeral had taken place, as he said that he could support his wife and other child much more effectively if he had some 'normality' around him. He said that he drew strength from the support of his colleagues. Also the physical break from the intensity of the sadness and grief in his home meant that he could come back from work with some energy to sustain himself and his family in their grief. As the perceived 'strong one of the family' Rob felt that his method of dealing with things was the only way he could cope. Alison and Rob recognised that they each had to deal with their grief in the best way for themselves and supported each other with their different reactions.

There is so much to deal with when you are in the depths of grief that you may find it difficult to know where to start. This is where our book comes in. We can help you to begin your journey and provide you with guidance and suggestions along the way. We never tell you what you ought to do, but share with you what in our experience we have found works.

So let's get started.

Most of all you need to act - moving forward requires that you actually **DO** move! We have come up with a series of actions that may help you. Which ones you start with depend on you, on how low you are feeling right now. You may have almost reached a state of hibernation, or you may be back at work. Choose one that feels right for you,

> **Choose an action that feels right for you**

one that makes you feel that you could do it, not that you should do it. To provide some sort of guidelines to the level of difficulty, in each chapter we have divided our suggestions into what we have called Baby Steps, Bigger Steps and Giant Strides.

The very first thing that you need to do is to look after your body. You need to care for the physical before you can deal with the rest. You need to look the part before you can act the part and then,

Look after your body

finally, live the part. So let's start there and find some ways that can help you to rejoin society. Think of the sorts of things that a mother might do for a child to show that she cares for them. Grief often reduces us to bewildered children and we need to show that child in us love and kindness. The first steps we suggest are some simple ways of looking after yourself. Where you start depends on how low you have become. Read through the list below and find one action that feels right for you. Or think of something similar that suits you. After all you know yourself best. We are not asking for a lifetime commitment to any of these actions, simply that you give one a go!

> **KEYPOINT ONE:** The first step on your journey is to look after your physical self.
>
> **KEYPOINT TWO:** Strengthening yourself physically **WILL** strengthen you emotionally.

ACTIONS

Baby Steps

- **Get up** – you may find that your sleep patterns are disturbed, that you are staying awake half the night and then lying in bed for most of the morning, or it may be that you just don't want to face another day. You **WILL** feel better if you get up. Providing yourself with something to think about other than your loss will give you some relief. Getting up is the first step to facing another day. That day is not going to go away, or wait until you feel in the mood for it. Once it's gone, it's gone. Don't lose this opportunity to start your journey forward now. Only you can do it.

- **Have a wash** – wash your face at least. Can you look at yourself in the mirror?

- **Get dressed** – rejoin society by putting something on so that you can mix with other people. There is a world out there and you can become part of it again.

- **Eat something** – if you don't look after your body, you will make yourself feel even worse. Food is your fuel to give your body strength to cope with facing the day. Without it you become even weaker and this will take its toll. Anything you can do to support your body at this time will contribute to your eventual healing.

Bigger Steps

- **Get up before 9am** – this is a way of making a statement to yourself and to other people that you are trying to live again. It will also help you sleep better because you will be properly tired when it is time for bed.

- **Have a shower –** a shower always makes you feel better, as long as it is a nice hot one. How about some of your favourite shower gel while you are at it?

- **Put on something you like -** this is a way of telling yourself that life still does matter and that you matter too.

- **Buy something new** – yes, go for some retail therapy. Whether it's a new T-shirt or a new gadget, at least it might take your mind off your grief for a few minutes while you decide what you want to wear or play with.

- **Go for a walk** – fresh air and exercise really are good for you. You will feel better afterwards and sleep better too.

- **Plan a nice meal and eat it** – again this is a way of reminding yourself that you are still here and you do still matter.

Giant Strides

- **Go out for a meal -** treat yourself, you're worth it!

- **Tidy up -** there is a temptation to make a physical shrine of the past. This is a way of removing that temptation and helping yourself to move forward.

- **Take up a new interest or extend a current one** – this is part of exploring who you might want to be. Your life is going to be different so why not use the opportunity to find out how different it could be? You might want to take up dancing or flying a kite – the choice is yours.

- **Grow something** – many people find solace in gardening. Neither of us can understand this but it does seem to help a lot of people!

CHAPTER TWO

THE REAL YOU

Who are you now?

Did you used to know who you were, before life dealt this blow? Can you ever remember feeling satisfied and secure within yourself? Can you remember a time

> **Can you remember a time when you felt good?**

when you felt good? Try and think of a moment in your life when you were happy. Think for a moment about how good you felt. Perhaps, on the other hand, you have never felt that way. Whatever your past experience, would you like to feel happier with yourself now?

The road of life does not run in a smooth straight line - and how boring it would be, if it did! Life's road is full of twists and turns. How often have we heard it said that, 'it's a good job we can't see what's around the corner,' as sometimes events happen that if we had known were about to happen, would have made us terrified. When bad things happen or when we are faced with grief, our whole way of being may alter. Some people describe themselves as 'in pieces' and some bereaved partners may say that they 'have lost half of themselves'.

Think about how you would describe yourself at this very moment. Do you feel as though you are in pieces? Do you feel bereft? Are you feeling relieved? Can you actually feel anything or would you describe yourself as being numb? There are so many ways each individual can feel and none of these feelings is wrong or inappropriate.

However you are feeling today, at this moment, this is how it is. This is where you are. Now think about how you

> **Imagine how you would feel, if you could choose**

would like to feel. Capture the feeling if you can, or try to imagine how you would feel, if you could choose. When you are broken or simply not feeling the way you wish you could be, there are options open to you. You can stay the way you are now and continue feeling and living like this. The way you are may actually be the only way of getting you through the initial stages of your grief and it may be right to continue being like this.

Grief happens and the feelings that come with grief are sometimes impossible to change at that time. The impact of grief can be all consuming and overwhelming and to put pressure on yourself to be any different is sometimes inappropriate and not beneficial. Changing how you are is a **CHOICE.** You do not even need to consider changing if you do not want to. What is good about having choice though is that, if the way you are is not working for you or for those around you, then you have an option. In other words, if the way you are is no longer serving you well, then maybe it is the right time to think about making changes. If you feel lost, lonely, heartbroken, raw or that life is now pointless, you are not on your own. One thing in this life is certain, and that is that we all will be hit by grief in some way, during our lives.

So - how are you going to deal with your loss? How are you dealing with it up until now? How have you reacted, what have you done so far and is what you have done working for you? Here is a list of how you may have reacted so far. Feel free to add anything personal to the list, and also tick off any of the suggestions that you know you have experienced or tried.

Common Reactions:

- Anger

- Depression

- Blame

- Loss of routine

- Overeating

- No appetite

- Poor sleep pattern

- Not sleeping

- Nightmares

- Sleeping too much

- Not wanting to go to bed

- Not getting dressed

- Not washing

- Apathy

- Avoiding contact with friends

- Avoiding people you know

- Turning down social invitations

- Loss of hope for future

- Not going to work

- Overworking

- Denial

- Avoiding discussion of what happened

- Not being able to talk about your loved one

- Feeling guilty

- Loss of confidence

- Not being able to look at photographs, video or DVD footage

- Not being able to think even about good times with your loved one

- Constantly wanting to talk about the person

- Drinking too much alcohol

- Crying

- Taking antidepressants

- Overworking

- Taking drugs

- Praying

- Fear of boring people

- Worry about burdening others

- Reduced self esteem

- Sadness

- Realisation of own mortality

- Fear for own health/fear of dying

- Fear of further loss

- Frustration

- Relief

- Anxiety of how you are going to cope

- Exhaustion

- Feeling overwhelmed

- Lack of concentration

- Loneliness

- Inability to plan

- Other _____

Rebuilding

You have now looked at some of the feelings and behaviours you may have adopted or experienced since your loss. Most of these experiences are the natural and normal result of grief and loss. It is healthy to work through these experiences and, with time, expect to come out the other side, feeling better and stronger than you do now.

What you are feeling and experiencing can bring you to **WHO** you want to be and **HOW** you want to be. It is possible to use your grief to rebuild your life the way you want it to be. Albert Einstein once said "The definition of insanity is doing the same thing over and over again and expecting

> **Do you want to change?**

different results". If you have been doing the same things over and over again and are not satisfied with the outcome, perhaps it is time to try something new. Are you happy with how you are? Would your loved one who has died, be proud of who and how you are today? If you think not, then do you want to change? Do you recognise yourself from the person you were before the bereavement?

You are you. There is no other you in the whole world! You are unique. There has never been a you before and there will never be another you, ever! Just stop. Think about this for a minute. **YOU ARE**

STILL IN THERE! You may be in pieces or feel only half there, but you can rebuild yourself, if you want to. If you decide to start rebuilding your life it is more positive not to look backwards at how you used to be. Aim instead to look forward and think about the future. You might be able to make this into an opportunity to build differently and you can build for the best. The person you have lost can be part of the build. You may feel that they have been very positive in your life, so why cut them out of your life completely? What a waste if you are to be lost in this loss. What a waste of the relationship you and your loved one had. How you are going to rebuild will depend on how you feel and where you are in your grief. If you can identify the essence of who and how you are now, then you know what you have got to start working with.

As a starting point, think about something good about yourself. We will call these good points 'attributes'. Think about your attributes. What is good about you? What are your strengths? Here is a list of suggested attributes. If you cannot recognise your attributes ask someone to tell you what they see as your good qualities.

Attributes:

- Considerate

- Kind

- Civil

- Decent

- Generous

- Entrepreneurial

- Thoughtful

- Honest

- Hard working

- Genuine

- Friendly

- Interested

- Funny

- Attractive

- Reasonable

- Clever

- Helpful

- Fair

- Efficient

- Happy

- Family orientated

- Good friend

- Brave

- Confident

- Accepting

- Mature

- Appreciative of others

- Able

- Reliable

- Powerful

- Punctual

- Practical

- Gets things done

- Gorgeous

- Flexible

- Loveable

KEYPOINT ONE: Recognising who you are now and how you would like to be is the important starting point to help you identify whether you want to change your life.

KEYPOINT TWO: You know what is best for your life.

ACTIONS

Baby Step

Please tick or circle any words from the list above that describe attributes you have or attributes other people have said you have.

This may help you realise and accept that the core of who you are is still in there. You have strengths and qualities that you can use to kick start your future. It may not seem like it at the moment, but it is possible to have a life worth living and to have a future that feels worthwhile and fulfilling.

Bigger Step

Now go through the list again and tick the attributes you would *like* to have.

The idea of doing this is to allow yourself to develop a vision of how you might like to be. This gives you something positive to work towards.

Giant Stride

Take one or two words from the list of attributes that you think might apply to you and say the word regularly, referring to yourself. Start believing in that small part of you. Hear yourself say the word and try to bring it into a conversation relating it to you. Write down any examples to support that you are, for example, **reliable.** Make a note of your thoughts and feelings so that you can look back over your work in the weeks and months to come.

Identifying yourself as an individual is important. You can over think or overdo, when really the most effective thing to do is **BE!** Be yourself. Remember - being yourself saves energy.

Debbie Moore and Carolyn Cowperthwaite

CHAPTER THREE

ME, OTHER PEOPLE AND GRIEF

What about other people?

The death of someone close to you has affected you deeply and the grief you are suffering can make you very self-centred. This is not surprising; indeed it is inevitable because grief strikes at your very heart. When you feel mortally wounded, you need to focus on dealing with that pain. It is difficult to think of anything else. But, however much you are wrapped up in your own pain, you need to remember that there are

> **Grief makes people do strange things**

other people who have been profoundly affected too. You may be the star of the show – the grieving wife/husband for example – but, without wishing to rain on your parade, this doesn't mean that you have the monopoly on grief. Other people related to that person too, they may have had significant connections with them, and they also have feelings. Remember this when these people are with you. You know that grief makes people do strange things – you've experienced that first hand after all – and it may make these people behave differently from usual. Grief is visceral, penetrating deep into our souls, triggering reactions and behaviour in our own lives that we can find hard to understand. This is happening to other people also, not just you. As well as being kind to yourself, you need to make allowances for other people.

What sort of allowances do you need to make for others? First, remember that most people mean well most of the time though they may have odd ways of

> **Most people mean well most of the time**

expressing it! If someone turns up on your doorstep with a tray of food, it doesn't mean that they think you can't cook. It may simply be a way of expressing a concern that they can't put into words, offering you comfort in the only way they know. Try to accept this help for what it is and remember that they may be grieving too. Just as other people are helping you, perhaps you in your turn can help them by allowing them to participate in some way in the grieving process, by allowing them to give that help. Don't automatically push people away – an all too common reaction when you are hurting so much. Perhaps instead you could even think of opportunities for them to help, if only in some small way, maybe getting some shopping in for you or picking up the kids from school.

The kindness of others can give you strength and interacting with others can lift you, however momentarily, out of that dreadful place you are in. Of course, this has to be balanced against the temptation to turn yourself into a victim who is dependent on others. It is important

> **There are still many good, kind people in this world**

that you get back to a normal life but there may be

bad days when you feel you really can't face the office, the school gate or the supermarket. Allowing someone to help you out then provides a gentle reminder that there are still many good, kind people in this world. In those circumstances, you are not being dependent; you are being kind to yourself and to others.

Secondly, bear in mind that these days not many of us are practised in dealing with grief. The conventions of the Victorian times, when people wore black and knew what they were supposed to do or say, have gone. We no longer have them to fall back on, and we can sometimes be clumsy in searching for ways to express ourselves. 'I'm sorry for your loss' may seem a stupid thing to say, almost as though you have simply mislaid the person who has died. Remember though that the intention is usually good. After all, what can anybody say in such a situation that doesn't sound trite? Appreciate the sentiment, even if you don't like the way it is expressed. There are, however, some people who do very much bring their own agendas with them. Such comments as 'It must be a relief that it's over' tell you a lot more about the person saying it than about the person to whom it is said. Don't forget, if a comment is clearly not well meant, then the problem is with the person saying it, not you. Dismiss from your thoughts what has been said and politely move away from the situation.

Some people do still have a lot of expectations about how someone who is grieving should behave. They can be quick to condemn if your method of dealing with your loss is to party at every opportunity and sometimes equally quick to condemn if you lock yourself away in your grief. There is no pleasing some people and you shouldn't even begin to try. The person you need to please is YOURSELF. In these

> **The person you need to please is YOURSELF**

circumstances, you need to recognise that these people have these expectations [they may not even realise how they are acting], but don't fall into the trap of feeling that you have to fulfil them.

Only you can know what is right for you in the end. You are the one who has to live your life and take responsibility for it and ENJOY it. This is your life and your journey.

What if I am one of 'the other people'?

On the other hand, you might be one of those other people. The person who has died may have meant a great deal to you but you may have little claim to a major part in their grief show. You may be grieving big time because that person was very important in your life but those around you don't expect you to be deeply affected and don't make allowances for you. You may even feel that you have no right to be affected so badly. Again, forget the conventions – if you are grieving then accept that. Be kind to yourself, even if no one else is! Develop strategies for working through your grief. The person who died was important to you. Acknowledge that importance by putting it into words. Write it

Be kind to yourself

down, get it out of your system and onto the page. This can help you to put things into perspective. It may help you to see that your grief is well founded, that your loss is significant. Though also do consider the possibility that you may have simply been tempted by the strange glamour of the grief bandwagon. For grief can lend importance to an otherwise humdrum life. Consider too whether you are actually grieving for your own life. The drama of death is a shocking reminder that we are all mortal, that life is fragile and that we need to make the most of it. If that's perhaps even partly the case, then still continue with this book. For later on we shall be looking at ways in which you can aim to achieve the life you want.

If the person who died was important to you, you may consider expressing that in a letter, phone call or Facebook message to the

Be honest with yourself

family, if appropriate. Be honest with yourself and examine your motives for what you do. Perhaps you could try writing down what you want to say and then show it to someone you trust before deciding whether to use it or not.

KEYPOINT ONE: Most people mean well most of the time. Don't take offence too easily.

KEYPOINT TWO: Be true to your essential self, whatever other people expect of you.

ACTIONS

Baby Steps

- **List three kind things that other people have done for you** – Counting your blessings like this not only reminds you that the world is not such a bad place but also means that, for a few minutes at least, you have respite from those black thoughts that may haunt you.

- **Think of one thing you could allow someone else to do for you** – think of all those offers of help that you have turned down. Choose one of them and give that person the opportunity to do it for you. For example, you could ask somebody if they could pick you up some bread and milk when they go to the supermarket.

Bigger Steps

- **Think of a kind action that you could do for someone else - and do it** – this acts as a gentle reminder that you are not the only one in the world who is going through difficult times. It also provides a distraction from your own worries.

- **Write or text three people thanking them for their support** – this doesn't have to be a major work of literature. A simple 'Thanks for your support' will do the job. It is the action of looking outside yourself which is important – and people do like being appreciated as well.

- **Start mixing with people again** – if someone has invited you for a cup of tea, take them up on the offer. Again, it will take you out of yourself, give you an opportunity to act like a normal human being, be another step on the road to recovery.

Giant Stride

- Think of one thing that you would like to do but you are worried about because of what other people will think. For example, you may be afraid of laughing, in case people think that you are over your grief and will no longer offer you their support. Do it, because you need to be yourself, not just a victim. Another example - if you are invited to a party and want to go - then go. Not going won't bring your loved one back and going might bring some ease at least for the moment.

Debbie Moore and Carolyn Cowperthwaite

SECTION 2

How are you?

Grief can give a great body blow to our confidence. Death is the ultimate proof that there are many things outside our control, However, death is also a great reminder that life is not a dress rehearsal. We only pass this way once so let's make the most of it. This section is about how

> **We only pass this way once**

you can provide yourself with the confidence to live the life you want. Yes, there are many ups and downs in life but we want to show you that there are things that you can do to make the most of the life you have now.

In Chapter Four, we recognise the need to grieve in our own ways but also consider the dangers of getting

> **The dangers of getting stuck in grief**

stuck in that grief and becoming a victim of it. We ask you to try to understand yourself and think about whether you are ready to move on.

In Chapter Five, we stand back for a minute to look at what life is about and our place in the greater scheme of things. We are all on our own particular journeys and some of them are exceptionally difficult. How we manage our journey can help us make the most of life.

Chapter Six looks at ways of learning to live again for those

Learn to live again

who are ready to move to the next stage in their lives.

CHAPTER FOUR

UNDERSTANDING

How you are coping with grief

What have you actually been through? Can you let yourself even begin to acknowledge what you have seen, lived through, felt and lost? Can you talk to anyone about what has happened? For so much of the time, in the first stages of grief, our brain is clever - it shuts down and only allows a small amount of detail to come to the surface at any one time. You may find you cannot think about what has happened. Looking at photographs may seem difficult or impossible. Alternatively, you may not be able to think about anything else. Your feelings of loss may be overwhelming and you might think you are 'losing it' or that you are becoming obsessed either with your loved one or the thoughts and feelings of loss.

People cope with grief in many ways. Some want to surround themselves with photographs and can even turn their home into some sort of shrine to the person who has died.

Sarah's boyfriend, Andy, died, aged 22, in a road traffic accident. Her reaction was to take the small photos she had of him to a photographer's to be enlarged and place them everywhere in her flat. She even wore a photograph in a necklace around her neck. She talked constantly about Andy to anyone and everyone who would listen and spent as much time as possible with his friends and family.

This way of grieving was not wrong for Sarah at that stage in her grief. It is how Sarah coped with the days and weeks after Andy's death. Remember, as we said in Chapter One,

THERE ARE NO RULES FOR GRIEF

We are all likely to react differently to our individual situations and, what is more, we all **NEED** to react in our own particular ways. Each one of us is a

> **We all need to react in our own ways**

unique human being in a unique set of circumstances. What works for one person is not going to necessarily work for another. Just as we can't wear each other's clothes, so we can't live each other's lives.

The Shutdown Mechanism

How you feel is part of how you are coping with what has happened. So what if you cannot feel how or what you think you should be feeling?

Graham had always expected that he would feel devastated by the death of his grandmother. He had dreaded the day that anything should happen to his grandmother because they were more like a mother and son. Because of this Graham felt that life would not be worth living if anything happened to her. His grandmother's death was quite unexpected and Graham had the news of it broken to him by his mum. He went to see a counsellor two weeks later because he could not feel any emotion regarding his loss. He had expected to cry and be overwhelmed with grief and yet he had carried on going to work and did not seem to feel anything.

What had happened to Graham was he had shut down immediately from the situation. He was not being unfeeling or uncaring. It was simply his body's way of coping.

This natural 'shutdown mechanism' protects us from some of the complete horror of what we are facing. We carry on living when maybe life does not feel like it should carry on at all. What is the point in carrying on, if we have lost so much? There is a natural response to pain and trauma that kicks in and can numb our consciousness from the reality of what is happening. Be aware of this shutdown mechanism and don't be afraid of it. If you are wondering how it is that you are able to function, how you are getting up each day, why you are not crying, then it may be this mechanism that is supporting you. If you run with this, grief is less likely to overwhelm you. You can face each part of your grief in a manageable way.

What if this mechanism has not kicked in? What if you are feeling overwhelmed? Cry, withdraw, sleep, be angry, scream, lack hope, be busy, do whatever you have to do to get through each minute. In the depths of despair, you have to be how you have to be! Let yourself be. Ask someone to be with you, if this will help.

Don't be afraid to ask for help. If you cannot think of anyone to ask, then telephone your G.P. or a

Don't be afraid to ask for help

bereavement agency. If you fear you are suicidal, the Samaritans can be contacted twenty four hours a day. Their local number will be in your phone book or online.

The famous singer Corin Bailey Rae, in an article written following the death of her young husband, said that she sat at the kitchen table and cried for the best part of a year. She totally withdrew from her work, friends and family and grieved. That was her choice and there was nothing wrong with that reaction. It was the most natural thing to do since she had lost the closest person to her, forever.

If you are grieving, it may be necessary to withdraw and experience the overwhelming pain that comes with loss. Don't forget though, that nothing ever stays the same. Something will change and you can claim some control as to how you are going to be in the future. Allow yourself time to be how you are naturally. Don't strive to move on before it feels right. You will know when the time comes, if the way you are grieving is not serving a purpose. You may be feeling helpless and even feel that you are in a rut. Your grief and the way you respond to it, may mean you can't do what you want to do. This rut can become a comfort zone and sometimes it feels easier and requires less energy to stay in that zone rather than dare to move out of it. You may feel safe in your grief as it means you can conserve energy to cope with your loss. Actually, this is what grief is about. It is about an individual's response to loss.

The comfort zone has its place but can turn from a natural protective mechanism, which is useful, to a zone which is not constructive or useful and indeed can become very limiting and even harmful to you. What then? How can you begin to take control and live the life you want to live? Are you feeling like a victim of circumstance? You may feel like a victim now,

Start thinking about how you want to be

but you can change that if you want to. Start thinking of how you want to be. You need to start planning! As with any successful change, there needs to be some planning in order to achieve a successful outcome. There is no magic wand but it is useful to set out small goals, so that you can measure whether you are progressing towards what you want to achieve.

Your thoughts are very powerful. They can make the difference between a bad moment and a good moment. Practising positive thoughts will help you develop a more positive outlook on life and this will benefit you and those around you.

James and Karen had two children both born with a congenital life-threatening illness. They had lived as a family with the day-to-day joy and worry that this type of situation can bring. Family life was never dull and the four members of this strong family unit lived life like any other family, with the added trials of regular hospital stays and exhausting treatment regimes. This family knew that time together was limited and each of them made sure that they enjoyed themselves as much as possible. Family holidays, shopping trips, meals out together and as much fun time together as possible was woven in to normal life. Their elder son, Matthew, died after being in hospital for a long time. Five weeks after the funeral their younger son, Liam, was taken suddenly into hospital. The doctors told them not to worry and that Liam should make a normal recovery, however he deteriorated and died suddenly two days later. Understandably, James and Karen were shocked and overwhelmed with grief. They had lost their two children within six weeks of each other. Karen no longer felt she had her role as Mum and James felt bereft. Family and friends rallied and expected the couple to fall apart completely. A year later the hospital nurse contacted the couple to check on how they were. James said that they were doing well in coming to terms with their loss. They had become involved in providing emergency foster care for young children as they felt that, as a couple, they had so much still to give. They realised through their grief that they wanted to find some purpose to their lives and they now look after these children in their own home.

Karen said that she and James are enjoying life and love being able to share their home with the children. As a couple, they realised that they had so much experience looking after their own children and they are able to use these skills in caring for the children sent to them.

James and Karen have said that they will never get over the death of their beautiful children, but through positive thinking and having worked through their grief they feel they have fulfilling lives.

KEYPOINT ONE: You know what you really need.

KEYPOINT TWO: Life can have enjoyable moments.

ACTIONS

Baby step

Write a list of anything you would like to do. Just writing this list may stimulate you into recognising that the items on the list may actually be possible to achieve.

Bigger step

Think about one particular goal you want to achieve and write it down on paper. Pin this to somewhere where you will notice it e.g. to the fridge, your bedroom mirror. Every time you see your goal, say it out loud, using the prefix 'I will and I can…'. An example of this is to write the words 'skydive' as your goal. When you see it, you will say out loud 'I will and I can skydive'. Training your mind to be positive about what is possible for you to achieve can lead to you working towards fulfilment of your goals and this will impact on your life.

Giant stride

Book your skydive (or whatever your goal is) and do it!!

Endnote

When you have achieved whatever it is you have set out to do, even the smallest of tasks, the important thing is to give yourself a huge 'pat on the back' for achieving your goal. This could take the form of ticking that item off the list you wrote for your Baby Step. The significance of the 'pat on the back' is that you remember to glean something positive from what you have done. These 'pats on the back' raise self-esteem and give us a feeling of pleasure and self-worth. As these small 'pats' accumulate, before we know it, more of these positive feelings begin to start creeping back in to the way we live our everyday lives.

CHAPTER FIVE

STUFF HAPPENS

The circle of life

In Chapter Four we talked about beginning to understand yourself, what has happened to you and how you are dealing with it. Chapter Five is about beginning to understand life, about how things happen and what we can do. We don't claim this is easy, but we do know it is something worth thinking about. We all need some sort of acceptance of what life is about to be able to manage what goes on in our lives, to be able to take responsibility and move forwards.

So, what are we getting at? To put it simply, everyone is going to die, nobody has an absolute

> **Anger can be very destructive**

right to anything in this life. **Life is not fair**. People we love die, sometimes in terrible circumstances.

We are left behind in pieces. This fact can be a source of great and ongoing anger. This anger can be very destructive; we can waste our energies looking back instead of building for the future. However, we can change our responses. We don't need to stay stuck in anger or despair forever. Life is too short and too precious to let our misfortunes prevent us from living life to the full. We have to learn somehow to acknowledge that life is indeed not fair and move on. Acceptance and the peace of mind that flows from that are of crucial importance in achieving this.

But how do we go about it?

Step one is to step back and recognize the circle of life, to accept the natural rhythm of birth and death. Most of us can do this most of the time. We may have had experience of an elderly relative or friend who has gradually faded and who is ready to die. And while we may have mourned for them, that mourning and grief has not overtaken and consumed our lives. We have been able to see this as a natural part of life. The difficulties mainly arise when death appears to come too soon. The father who doesn't get a chance to see his children grow up, the child who never has the chance to blossom into an adult, a life cut short through someone else's carelessness or sheer bad luck – they can all be a source of terrible unremitting grief and anger. How can anyone deal with, never mind accept, such obscenities?

Stuff happens

Stuff happens. It can be good stuff or bad. There is lots of stuff that could happen to us and doesn't. Yes, something terrible has happened and there is nothing you can do about that. It is in the past and cannot be undone. All we ever have is the here and now and that is the only place where we can make a difference. How we live every moment is a matter of personal choice and responsibility. In the end

only we can choose how we feel. Other people may
do things to us or say

> **Only we can decide what is important to us**

things about us, they may
leave us or never leave us
alone but they cannot dictate our responses. Only
we can decide what is important to us.

We choose these people and then they go and die on
us! How unfair is that? But think for a moment what
they have given us. Would we grieve so dreadfully,
if they hadn't given us so much? And this is where
we need to rethink how we see things, to establish a
balance between the bad and the good memories.
For it can seem in the depths of grief that all that is
left is a bundle of searingly painful memories of the
process of dying and the loss. These memories can
completely overwhelm us and are the reason why
we feel that pain. This is when we need to start
remembering the good times too. That can be
painful in itself because our loved ones aren't there
any more but isn't there some comfort and
happiness we can get from them?

Stuff is always going to happen. You cannot prevent it or make it go away. All you can do is manage your reaction to it in the way that you want to. Some of us like to think long and hard about what has happened, we want to grieve big time and get it over with. Others of us find that too overwhelming, we have to hide our grief away and carry on functioning, perhaps fearing that if we stop we may never function again, ever. No way is right or wrong in itself, only right or wrong for you.

The problems can come when grief makes you sick to the stomach, unable to function, adopting avoidance tactics. There may come a point when you need to face it head on, deal with it and move on. Only you are responsible for your reactions and only you can change them. Of course many of our reactions are instinctive, visceral even. We may not be able to stop ourselves feeling sick to the stomach but we can work at managing that sickness, perhaps by trying to eat a little, perhaps by finding distractions. There is a difference between the immediate reaction and ongoing behaviour. We are only human and are creatures of habit. It is only too easy to get into the habit of grieving. Any habit is has its comforts and can be difficult to kick, no matter how distressing it is, because part of that habit is that we know what

Changing habits is scary

happens and so we feel safe. Changing habits is scary and it requires lots of practice to create a new and much better habit.

We don't claim to offer answers, merely to say that this may be worth thinking about. We don't know why the good or the bad stuff happens, we just know that it does. We can't undo what has happened but we can examine our responses to it and decide whether we want to try to change them. We are all on our own particular journeys, some a lot trickier than others.

> **KEYPOINT ONE:** Stuff happens, good and bad. We can't control that but we can take charge of how we react to it.
>
> **KEYPOINT TWO:** All we have is the here and now. Make the most of it.

ACTIONS

Baby Step

Count one blessing in your life right now. Write it down. Keep reminding yourself of it throughout the day. Thinking about even one blessing will lift your mood.

Bigger Step

Be your own spin doctor. Write, text, tweet or Facebook something good that has happened today. Looking for the positive makes you feel more positive generally.

Giant Stride

Write, paint, draw or record the story of what has happened to you. Pick out good bits and add some more detail about them.

CHAPTER SIX

LEARNING TO LIVE AGAIN

Losing someone you love means learning to live in a different way. Life will not be the same again. Would you expect it to be? You can't bring someone back following their death, and you cannot live life exactly as before, because put simply, your loved one is not with you to live life as you did before.

Pain may be constant at the moment and you may be finding it difficult/ impossible to bear. How do people continue to live with the raw pain of grief? Pain

Learn how to manage your emotions

of loss may never go away, but it is possible to learn how to manage the emotions that loss brings. The following technique is something you may find useful as a tool to help you cope with the pain of loss.

The Pain Box

Imagine that the pain box is an invisible box that sits inside your mind. Stay with the idea for the moment while we explain. As you get used to a feeling or once you have dealt with an emotion, you can choose to throw it away/let go of it or you can, in your imagination place the painful feeling into the pain box. This imaginary box has a lid on it and it can be locked shut and placed neatly on an imaginary shelf in your mind. Once you have metaphorically placed a thought or feeling into the box you can shut off from it. For example, you may decide to put angry thoughts about a situation in to the box. You can then use your energy to concentrate on something else. You may be able to fall asleep, go to work or watch a television programme and not having to deal with the angry thoughts for that moment could be helpful. This box is useful as you can use it whenever you wish. You can lift the lid whenever you want to and revisit feelings as and when you want. You can also use the box to put away feelings that you are not ready to cope or deal with. You may want to talk to someone you trust about this theory and plan how best you can use it. Using this tool in a way that suits you means you can free some time and energy to get on with your day to day coping. You can gain some peace of mind and calm, which can then help you to deal with what's ahead of you.

Jim, a 56 year old, had been dreading the wedding of his youngest daughter since his wife had died six months earlier. He did not want to go to the wedding because he was worried that he would break down in tears during the ceremony. He came for counselling and the pain box theory was introduced to him as a possible tool for him to use. He talked it through and over a period of several weeks began practising placing emotions and thoughts into the 'pain box'. A week after the wedding he came for a session and said that not only had he managed to get through the wedding without a tear, but he had thoroughly enjoyed himself! He had promised himself beforehand that he would take time the following day to revisit the box and think about whatever he wanted to. He was able to control his feelings and emotions on the day of the wedding and the process enabled him to experience the fun of the here and now. His daughter had her wedding and was able to enjoy her Dad being there.

To take the theory a step further, you can create another imaginary box called a joy box. This box can sit on the shelf and it can be used to put any pleasurable memories, moments of laughter, feelings of love, funny times, in fact anything positive can be placed there. The importance of having these two boxes at your disposal means you can start to learn to control your emotions and even learn to enjoy life again. Being able to store feelings and emotions means you don't have to let go of anything before moving on. It can speed up the healing process and when you feel a little stronger you can decide when to lift the lid to face, at your own pace, issues that you want to deal with. No one is more in tune with how you feel, more than you are. This is the reality and yet you can learn to live again. Life is worth living.

There can be some comfort in life not being the same and many people say that they never want life to be the same. Some people feel that to try and live the way they did before their loss would be a backward step. It may be that you feel that you will never enjoy life again. When we grieve, we do not view our life in the way that we did before we were grieving. In simple terms, you will need to reorganise the way you live life. It is never going to be the same, but with help and work, life can be fun and happy at times. It may be that you decide to create new patterns within the way you live. For example, change where you go on Christmas Day, go somewhere on holiday that you have never been to before. Cook different meals, invite a friend to go for a drink in a pub you have never been to. Use your imagination to look for different ways to change what you do. This can be energising and you may find that you start to enjoy some of what you do. Action works!

New traditions/patterns can make things not only bearable, but at times, wonderful. On the other hand, you may find great comfort in the familiarity and warmth of traditions you built up with your loved one. You do not have to change anything. Choose the way that suits you best.

Positive words can give hope. Realising others are grieving and watching how they cope may be helpful. You never know, one day, it could be that the way you have carried on may be someone else's inspiration!

Your future will feel uncertain, unhappy and even pointless and hopeless. These feelings are normal and you will need to have time to work through them. So where are you now? Are you living the life you want? Are you as happy as you could be? Are you looking forward

> **Are you as happy as you could be?**

to the future? This is your life. You live once and only you can make the most of your life. Where can you start? Start at the very beginning! This may be a time for you to take stock and assess where you are with your life. Some people will never have the insight or will to do this and yet you can take this opportunity, since a life changing event has occurred, to live your life in as fulfilled way as possible. This may seem impossible especially if you are hurting, however it can be done. You can learn to live again.

Change

Do you want to change? If not that is fine. You may

want to stay feeling as you are and continue living as you are because you feel that this is the way you want to live. Is how you are hindering you or anyone around you in any way? This is something you may want to consider. How we are affects those around us. Taking notice of how you are affecting others may give you reason for wanting to change. Perhaps look out for signals that all is not well with yourself. Are you sleeping well? Do you wake in the early hours? Are you motivated to do what you want to do? Do you cry a lot? Are you absent from work regularly?

Once we start to look at our lives and how we impact on others we can more easily decide whether we want to change. If you genuinely don't want to or don't feel the need to live in a different way, then you can always reassess at a future point in time and wait until you are ready. If however you do want to live a more fulfilling existence, then there are steps you can take NOW! You have established how you are living, now you can make a start on how you want to live. It can be helpful to write down any issues you feel that you have right now that may be holding

> **There are steps you can take now**

you back from living your life. Once you have identified issues you can then decide what to **let go of** and what **needs to be dealt with**. Anything can be put in these two groups. Think about it for a minute. How you want to be may not be possible at the moment. Let's do an exercise. For the purpose of this exercise, lets call how you want to be, your **golden life**. Anything that gets in the way of your golden life means that you need to let go of it or deal with it. To move forward you must only keep thoughts and behaviors that keep you moving toward your goal of living a golden life.

Jane was angry at the death of her partner. She could not move on and although she wanted to become a teacher she was too occupied with her anger over her partner's death. Once Jane acknowledged what her goal was, she then identified what was blocking her progress. She knew her anger would not bring her partner back. She also knew that being angry was draining and it was affecting not just her, but her whole family. Jane decided she could not throw her anger away, it was too deep for this to happen, so in keeping with this exercise her other option was to deal with what was holding her back. She asked her GP for a referral for counselling and spent several sessions working on how to deal with the anger she was experiencing. Jane went on to apply to train as a teacher and is about to qualify. She has since said that her life is so fulfilled and she recognizes that her partner's death has led to something very positive. Life will never be the same without him. Life is different, but life has purpose. Jane says that she looks forward now and never back. Not a moment goes by that she doesn't think of her partner and she knows how proud he would be that she has continued to live her life in such a positive way.

As with any physical exercise, practice makes perfect and, as with physical training, the more you do, the stronger you become,. With emotional exercises you can become stronger, the more you practise.

KEYPOINT ONE: Action works. Do something.

KEYPOINT TWO: You have a future. Aim to make it the best it can be.

ACTIONS

Baby Steps

- Identify one simple thing you would like to do today.

- Do it and allow yourself to feel proud that you have done what you said.

Bigger Steps

- Identify three tasks you want to do in the course of a week.

- Plan when and how you will do these tasks.

- Do your tasks within the timescale set, i.e. a week.

- Allow yourself a treat for achieving your goal.

Giant Strides

- Write down one small goal that you would like to work on.

- Write down any reasons why you can't achieve the goal.

- Divide your list into two sections headed 'deal with' and 'let go of'.

- Make plan on how to deal with each reason. (Get help from friend, family or ask your GP to be referred for counselling)

- Achieve your goal.

SECTION THREE

What are you going to do?

You may have come to the point where you feel ready to take action. The first task is to find a focus for that action. For that, you need to ask yourself the big question – what do you want to do with the rest of your life? We discuss strategies for getting rid of the self-defined limits that we so often impose and ways of starting to take steps, however small, that will eventually carry you through your grief and on to a new life.

Chapter Seven starts with the question 'What shall I do?' and shows how we need instead to consider what we **WANT** to do, to start thinking about the future. We are the ones who

> **What do you want to do?**

know ourselves best and who know what is best for us but we can also listen and learn from others that we trust.

In Chapter Eight we look at how to find the energy to move forward by identifying and then overcoming the barriers that stand between us and the lives we want to live. A more detailed framework for action is suggested in the Living through Grief model,

A framework for action

providing a clear structure to follow to achieve your goals.

In Chapter Nine we look back briefly over all that we have discussed. We then turn to the many

Moving forward

reasons that there are for moving forward and finally look ahead to the possible futures that you could enjoy.

CHAPTER SEVEN

WHAT SHALL I DO?

What shall I do?

This is a question that you may have lost the answer to. Before the death of this significant person in your life you may have well known what to do. Your future may have been bound

> **Where do you go from here?**

up with that person. You may have had the responsibility of looking after them or they may have even been responsible for looking after you. That has all gone now. You can never get it back. So where do you go from here?

The problem is that if you ask 'What shall I do?', this question passes the responsibility for your actions on to somebody else. You are asking other people for guidance on how you should live your life. However, what we have learnt over these last few chapters is that the best person to tell you what is right for you is YOU. Nobody else knows you as well as you know yourself. No one else knows your innermost desires and fears as well as you do. This is the time to take responsibility for your own life, if you haven't already done so. And so the question changes from 'What shall I do?' to 'What do I want to do?'

What do you want to do?

'Want' is often regarded as a very selfish word. Children are told off for saying 'I want…'. We are taught to consider others but first of all we have to love ourselves and in loving ourselves, we have to value our own particular desires – providing of course that they cause no harm to anybody else. Another way of asking the question might be 'What is right for you?' However, the idea of 'right' is a tricky one. What is right for one person may be entirely wrong for another. We can get caught up in ideas of what we ought to do. It is all too easy to import other people's ideas of what is right, whereas if we ask what we want then it is much more straightforward.

We do all have many different and sometimes conflicting wants. A desire to put your feet up and watch the TV for three hours while consuming a large box of chocolates or six cans of lager may conflict with a desire to wear skinny jeans or play football. So really what we are asking when we say 'What do you want?' is 'Describe how you would like your future to be.' It is only when we have developed a clear vision of our future that we can begin to

> **How would you like your future to be?**

work towards it. The vision provides us with a goal or set of goals and once we have those then we can begin to map out a route which will take us there. Only then can we work out the individual steps that we need to take day by day and only then do we have the reason and drive for taking those steps because they will lead us where we want to go.

Remember, you can change your life, if you really want to. First you need to decide what you want to achieve and you need this to be as clear as possible. There are lots of ways of doing this. One way is to think back on times when you felt happy in yourself. Why was that? Was it because you were with a great bunch of people? Maybe it was because you had solved a particularly knotty problem? These are all clues to the direction you might want to go in. On the other hand, you may have always cherished a secret dream, or even a not so secret one, of doing something that is way outside all your previous experience. Perhaps you have always dreamt of being a pilot? Then how about getting together the money to have a single lesson ? It might inspire you to greater heights or make you realise that you really don't like it in which case you can move on to something else. Another technique is to get a pile of magazines and without pausing for thought rip out images that appeal to you. Make a collage of the results and see what strikes you. Are they all images of gardens? Perhaps you are trying to tell yourself something?

Secondly, you don't necessarily need to work out the route to getting there all at once. You don't have to carry out the whole of your plan in one go. You can do, of course but you may find it helps, at least in the beginning, to work out a few 'baby steps' and take those first. Then work out a few more.

The next step is to check whether your plan is working for you. Don't just rely on your own assessment. Many of us are extremely self critical and will find it difficult to

Check whether your plan is working for you

recognise the progress we have made. Ask a friend you can trust for their opinion. You might say that you haven't achieved your target. They might point out that you have got far closer to it than you might ever have imagined even a few months before.

If your plan isn't working then you haven't failed, you have simply learnt something, that it is the wrong plan for you right now. Make some changes or throw away the old plan and devise an entirely new one in the light of what you have learnt and try again. Look at it this way, you probably feel you have lost everything, so there is nothing more to lose. Give it a go.

Mentors and Role Models

Although we have warned against merely following what other people think you should do, we are not against asking for advice. On the contrary, we can gain valuable insights from asking other people about possibilities. For example, perhaps you are thinking of resigning from your job. By all means work out a list of the pros and cons, reasons for and against leaving your job. In fact, that's what you need to do to help you understand your own thinking. But perhaps it might also be an idea to talk to someone you can trust. Ask them what they think, if they can see anything that you may have left out. You don't necessarily have to take their advice but it may be a good idea to listen to what they have to say.

Sometimes we don't even have to talk to the people who can help us. The example of their lives can provide us with a role model. Perhaps there is someone you admire, who you think is leading the sort of life you might like to live. What are the particular qualities in them that you admire? Are they qualities you would like to have? Can you think of ways of developing those qualities in your own life?

KEYPOINT ONE: You are the person who knows you best.

KEYPOINT TWO: Develop a vision of the future you want as a goal to work towards.

ACTIONS

Baby Steps

- Write down one simple want that you have today.

- Describe three very small steps you could take towards achieving that want.

Bigger Steps

- Think about something you would like to do in a month's time.

- Work out three steps you could take towards achieving it.

Giant Strides

- Describe a day in the life you would like to have five years from now.

- List ten significant actions you could take to help you achieve that day.

Debbie Moore and Carolyn Cowperthwaite

CHAPTER EIGHT

WHAT CAN I DO?

What can I do?

You **can** do anything you want to do - how liberating! Nothing is out of your reach; it is a matter of realising what it is you want and then working out **how** you are going to do

> **Realise what it is you want**

it. This takes energy to do and finding the energy or creating the energy is the starting point. Nothing can change what you have been through but you can change how you deal with the situation. You can be in control and lead your life in a fun and meaningful, even successful way. What are you good at? What do you enjoy doing? Can you dream about how you would like your life to be? Do you like who you are? Do you like who you have become? Can you find the real you inside the pain? Can you identify that you are still in there? How do others see you?

We talked earlier in Chapter 6 about learning to live life again. Managing to do that may be the first step on the road to recovery, to regaining some control over your life. In Chapter 7 we moved on to talking about making a plan for your future in general terms. Now in Chapter 8 we offer a framework for this plan that you might find helpful.

Perhaps there are barriers in the way of you achieving what you can and want out of life. Let's have a look at what these barriers might be and identify how you can not only overcome them, but actually banish them from your reality. Banishing barriers allows us to conserve energy which we can then use to facilitate change and edge further towards achieving our goals. We have created what we call The Living Through Grief Model. This provides you with a series of steps, a clear way of structuring your action plan to achieve your goal, whatever it is. Why don't you pick a simple goal that you would really like to achieve and try using this model to help you?

Let's begin with an outline of the model.

The Living Through Grief Model

1. Identify a goal

2. Identify barriers

3. Banish barriers

4. Conserve/generate energy

5. Start Baby Step plan

6. Move to Bigger Step plan

7. Take Giant Strides

8. Enjoy your Catwalk moment!

To use this model, you begin by identifying your goal. This can be something simple or a more challenging one. Using the model can help you take a step approach and will increase your chance of achieving your goal. The last step of the model is called the catwalk moment. This term is used to describe the moment when you achieve what you set out to do. To use the analogy, when a model walks down the catwalk of a fashion show, this is the model's moment of glory. All the hard work preparing for the ultimate walk comes to fruition and the cameras roll and the audience cheer. Everything the model has worked towards is on show and the peak of the experience occurs on the catwalk, both for the audience and the model.

Here is an example of someone grieving, who used the model, which eventually led to her achieving something she wanted to do.

Jenni, a thirty six year old, was grieving following the death of her best friend, Rosie. Her friend had died suddenly in tragic circumstances and Jenni was experiencing extreme anger over her loss. She was angry about so much of what had happened, angry to have lost her friend, angry at the fact that she had been unable to stop the suicide from occurring, angry with some of her other friends as they had argued with Rosie only days before her death. Anger, anger and more anger! In fact Jenni was spending most of her time and energy being angry. She could not understand why she felt that way so much of the time. During a counselling session, Jenni was able to acknowledge that all her anger was not going to bring back her friend. The only person suffering as a result of these negative feelings was herself.

In her counselling session she was introduced to the Living Through Grief Model. She decided to try the model and started with the simple goal of getting a voluntary job. This is how she used the model.

1. Goal:

- *Voluntary job, one day a week.*

2. Barriers:

- *Tiredness due to not sleeping, as she was often angry at night.*

- *Lack of willingness to be pleasant to people.*

- *Fear that she would not be able to concentrate to do the job.*

3. Banishing barriers:

- *Sleep plan - where she made a list of what to do, e.g. make a herbal tea, if she couldn't sleep.*

- *Practising being nice to family and friends for short periods.*

- *Accepting that it would be possible to leave the job if she did not feel that it was working.*

4. Conserving/generating energy:

- *Plenty of rest.*

- *Starting gentle exercise.*

- *Seeing friends who make her feel relaxed and happy.*

5. Baby Steps:

- *Discuss goal with someone she can trust, perhaps a family member, friend or counsellor.*

- *Look at what jobs are available.*

6. Bigger Step plan:

- *Apply for a job with the help of the job centre.*

7. Giant Strides:

- *Attend interview and ask questions to ensure that the job is appropriate.*

8. Catwalk moment:

- *Charity shop work- **DONE!***

- *Made new friends- **DONE!***

- *Structure to week- **DONE!***

- *Reason to get up in the morning- **DONE!***

KEYPOINT ONE: Setting goals leads to action.

KEYPOINT TWO: You can have a catwalk moment!

ACTIONS

Baby Step

Write down one small goal. It can be anything you want.

Bigger Step

Work out what you need to do to follow the Living Through Grief model with the goal you have set as your baby step.

Giant Stride

Do it!!!!

CHAPTER NINE

THE WAY AHEAD

We hope this book has helped you at least a little. We have both had our own personal experiences of grief and are still living with the consequences of it years later. We have also lived, worked and walked with many other people who have had their own journeys through grief and learnt a lot from them. We are ordinary human beings simply trying to make the best of our lives. We don't claim to have all the answers but we have taken what has helped us and helped many other people and shared it with you. We have written from the heart to share our thoughts. Our goal is not to provide all the answers but to use our own and others' experiences and knowledge to help you get to the other side of grief.

At the end of the day, however, how you live the

life you have is your choice – and yours alone. There will be circumstances you cannot change and at the same time you have experienced a great loss which has changed your life forever. What you can change, if you want, is how you deal with those circumstances and that loss so that you can live the life you want.

We all die, sometimes sooner rather than later. When you reach the end of your life will you think of your life as worthwhile? Did losing someone ruin your life or was your life better because they were part of it?

How you live will affect others around you. You may have family or friends who need to be able to enjoy time with you. How do others see you now? Do they see someone who is living life to the full? Are you a victim of grief? Grief can overwhelm us and turn us into someone we do not want to be. Think again of the person who has died. What a credit and honour to them, if you can manage to carry on with life with courage and strength. Being able to smile again, to have fun and even enjoy moments of life would be such an incredible tribute to the person you have lost.

We have said from the start of the book that how you are dealing with grief is sometimes out of your control and we have given suggestions on how to look after your physical self, whilst the emotional side of your personality is hurting and unstable. The effects of your grief may have left you feeling ravaged and it may feel that you will never get any ease to the pain and despair that you feel.

How can you now ensure that you move towards living life the way you want to live?

Life will not be the same for you again. You will not get your 'old' life back. You won't feel the same as you did again. This means you won't go through experiences in the same way again either. There can be some comfort in that. Grief moulds our life into something different. It changes things. Change can bring opportunity. Opportunity can lead to positive outcomes. Living with grief can be made more bearable by running with the change and ensuring that any positive opportunity is taken.

You may find a new friendship or notice acts of kindness from others. You may be able to begin to think of your positive memories as something special and precious. Remember, each memory is unique to you and can be very much part of your new life. It may be that your memories become central to your rebuild of your life, the foundation stones of your new build. These memories never have to go. They are yours to own and no one can take them from you. You don't have to explain them; you can draw on them whenever you want and you never have to let them go.

We have offered various ideas throughout the book and believe that they can have a positive effect on your way of living. Don't be too hard on yourself if you find that you hit times when you just can't make the changes you want to. Sometimes grief can get a hold and it is not possible to control the feelings and symptoms that hit you. Remembering you know some theories, that you can have access to tools to help you, may get you back on track more quickly. There is sometimes nothing to lose by trying out different techniques and potentially you have something to gain.

Wouldn't it be amazing if you could enjoy your life again? You can have fun. You can laugh again. You can make new friends or enjoy the company of your old friends and family. You can work, have holidays, relax, enjoy good food, and walk in the sunshine. This is your life and you can be the best you have ever been. Guilt often holds people back from experiencing life to the full when someone they love has died. Some say it would be offensive to move on, as it would mean they did not care enough for the person. There is an alternative which is to let go of the guilt and ensure that positive memories are incorporated, to ensure that the person who has died is thought about just as much and is part of your new life. How much better for you to have a life well lived in memory of someone who has meant so much to you. You can do it. It takes courage, but you can find that. Think of what you have faced so far and you are still here, trying to carry on. Be proud of you. You may never accept what has happened and that is OK. It is more than OK, it is your right. You can decide to make sure though that you are the best you can be. You can decide that death is not going to destroy the life you now have. You can rise above the negative of what has happened and move to a positive state. You can have a great life and after all you have been through - you deserve it!

Enjoy! We wish you well. Take hold of life. Treasure memories; embrace courage, physical care, friends, family, tools, theories and planning. Remember to be yourself. It's OK to cry, its OK to laugh, work, smile, have fun. You are the only you there is.

LIVE THE BEST LIFE YOU CAN

ABOUT THE AUTHORS

As a Clinical Nurse Specialist and qualified counsellor, Carolyn worked with terminally ill people for 20 years. She set up a bereavement programme, working with parents, partners, siblings, extended family members and friends.

Debbie, a former teacher, has a background in academic research, being qualified to PhD level. She has worked in many areas of education.

15872123R10066

Printed in Great Britain
by Amazon